Fa

The Eternal Word,
the One God, the Free Spirit,
speaks through Gabriele,
as through all the prophets of God—
Abraham, Job, Moses, Elijah, Isaiah,
Jesus of Nazareth,
the Christ of God

Father Words
for You, too

Words of the Eternal to His child,
given through the prophetess
and emissary of God,
Gabriele

Gabriele
Publishing House

"Father Words for You, too"

3rd Edition, July 2024
© Gabriele-Verlag Das Wort GmbH
Max-Braun-Str. 2, 97828 Marktheidenfeld, Germany
www.gabriele-verlag.com
www.gabriele-publishing-house.com

Translated from the original German title:

„Vaterworte auch an Dich"

The German edition is the work of reference
for all questions regarding the meaning of the contents.

Order No. S108MIEN

Printed by:
KlarDruck GmbH, Marktheidenfeld, Germany

ISBN 978-3-96446-576-4

Preface

Words of guidance.

Words from the eternal universal life, from the source of truth, the fullness of the All-power, from the highest consciousness of the universe.

With this small book we are privileged to share in the personal words of the Father for His child. These words are also directed to us, to accept and receive in us.

According to the will of the Lord, His prophetess, Gabriele, lets us share in the gifts from the Spirit of God, which she was privileged to receive as His child. Let us accept thankfully what the Almighty also wants to say to us.

Gabriele-Verlag Das Wort
Gabriele Publishing House - The Word

I Am with you

Come to Me at every moment. Talk everything over with your Father whose spirit dwells in you. I, the Life, want to lead and guide you.

Wherever you are, there Am I, for I dwell in you and in all Being.

Let your heart continuously radiate love, then you are linked with Me, with the One who I Am in all forms of life, the Spirit of your Father.

Do not fear

I your Father, Am the love.
You came forth from My eternal consciousness. The consciousness of eternal life is also your life.

See, you do not die.
What should die is your human ego, your passions and base tendencies. The more these die, the more I will resurrect in you.

If I Am then consciously resurrected in you, and you become aware of Me, then you truly live.

I will resurrect in the one who resur-rects in Me, and he will be with Me consciously, and I with him.

This, My child, is the true life, far from oppressing fear, from sin and death.

Do not sin

y child, sin is against your heavenly Father.

Everything that does not correspond to My holy law is sinful. The one who loves Me keeps My commandments; he fulfills the law of life.

If you truly love Me, you will see to it that your feelings, thoughts and words are pure, that your actions are good and your life selfless.

Then your being will be filled with light. The beauty of your inner being will then find expression externally. You will gain in charm and spirituality.

Then you will become a being that is permeated by My sublime and noble light, by a power of light that radiates, that shines through you and illuminates your neighbor.

This is the pure love, My child, which sets you free. Sin binds the soul and keeps it in the imprisonment of human thinking and wanting.

Divine love makes you free and beautiful.
It marks the person through the nobility of a pure soul.

*Become pure
and you will be free*

My child, the purity of the soul makes the person virtuous and good.

The one who loves, gives, and the one who gives becomes free.

See, the giving one is truly free from everything that is dear and precious to the one who takes. The giver has only to look into the countenance of the taker to recognize what the latter needs. Therefore, give to the one who is in need and at the same time you are giving yourself to Me, the eternal Giver.

The Giver is very near to the one who gives; it is the love, which frees the soul from the ties of greed, envy and egoism.

My child, only the giving one has true freedom. Give and you receive love and freedom from Me. In selfless giving, the selfless seeker finds the justice of the Father who knows how to protect and sustain His child.

See the sparrows; they do not gather and reap; they do not gather in barns, yet they are sustained and are free, through the giving, all-just Spirit.

See the lilies in the fields; they flourish without asking why it rains and from where the waters flow that give them to drink.

Oh see, they sense the All-justice, the giving life, the I Am in all Being.

Be just to yourself

I Am the Love, the All-just Spirit. Become just yourself, then you will find your way to Me, the Love.

See, I lead you by way of your base feelings and thoughts, by way of your words that often do not correspond to your feelings and thoughts. How often does a person speak other than he thinks. This is hypocrisy and is not honest. See, My child, in this lies the conflict that does not let the person become free and loving. The hypocrite is not clever; he wants to cover up what is nevertheless evident to Me. Although he has put himself in the best light before his neighbor for the moment, the One who knows about all things will let all things become evident, according to the law of sowing and reaping.

Be just to yourself. Speak only what you feel and think.

If you have made this a part of you, then, My child, you will observe yourself more and more each day, and you will surrender everything that is impure to the redeeming light of your Father, so that your cast of mind may become noble and your feelings and thoughts good.

If your cast of mind is noble, then you will speak only what is noble and good. Because when your cast of mind marks your feelings and thoughts, then your feelings and thoughts are the same as your words.

See, this is the justice to yourself.

A good attitude leads to good doings and dealings

The person who thinks only the good and noble will also engage in good trade. See, My child, in the temporal there are business transactions, but not in the eternal life.

A person needs many a thing which the soul has already long since possessed as a gift from the Giver of eternal life.

A person needs food and clothing, shelter and many other things. The soul, which possesses the wealth of the heavens in itself, must often patiently endure what the shell, the person, needs, what he aspires and strives for.

Selfless business transactions contain at the same time a positive way of life. The one who carries out trade in the spirit of selfless love will also walk in Me, the All-justice.

See, only the one who is noble and pure and like Me, the Eternal One, has a clear conscience. A good attitude over the course of time liberates both person and soul.

Freedom

y child, to be free means to be free of oneself.

What does being free mean? When a person's aspiration and striving is to please only God, he will not take the opinion of his neighbor and make it his own. He will not take the longings and desires of his neighbor and make them his own. His longing consists in pleasing God, so that he may grow ever closer to Me, the Eternal.

See, in self-complacency lies overestimation, an overvaluation of one's own person. This results in a human kind of contentment.

But this self-satisfaction brings the spiritual life to a standstill, and thus, constriction and lack of freedom.

May the one who wants to be free look only to Me and be single-minded in spirit. May he not be lukewarm. To be lukewarm is to fall away from Me and opens the way for personality thinking.

To be free means to be one with Me in word and in deed. This is truly the seed that brings a good harvest both for the God-person and for his neighbor, My child.

The good seed

My child, the true life is giving. Therefore, to give is better than to take. To give sets soul and person free.

In giving lies relinquishment, the self-sacrifice, the sacrifice of all that is dear and precious to a person.

See, the selfless gift in word and deed is the good seed that will bear fruit. The fruit will not be given back to the Earth, for a ripe fruit always finds its taker. It is the Spirit of life, which harvests the ripe fruit and brings it into the land of maturity, the land of eternity, where only fully matured life has its place.

Become ripened fruit

The one who wants to mature on the tree of recognition must make sacrifices, not only for his own sake, but for the common good. For one bears the burden of the other.

The soul matures in self-recognition, My child.

Self-recognition and the sacrifice of your self are not sufficient to enable you to enter the Father's house. Only the voluntary sacrifice of love for one's neighbor, the voluntary, selfless act of love, serving others, opens the door to eternal consciousness for the soul, to Me, to the One, who I Am, the Life.

The sacrifice of love for one's neighbor

The selfless sacrifice of love done in the right way, that is true life. It frees the soul from the shackles of its ego.

Through this, person and soul find access to all those hearts that truly seek Me.

A sacrifice of love means to give up your self, to think no more of yourself, to no longer demand or crave, to give yourself only to God and to your neighbor.

That is true sacrifice; that is the greatness of consciousness.

The one who surrenders himself self-lessly gains more than he can imagine. I will be with him and give him what he needs and what is good for soul.

True greatness

My child, greatness is shown only by the one who forgets his self. And the one who has forgotten his self is great.

How small and lowly is the human ego, the person, whose thinking and acting revolve only around his own interests, who is concerned solely with his own welfare.

See, what you think and do today are the seeds for tomorrow. Therefore, the rich person who strives only for his own welfare and possessions will, depending on his way of life, gradually lose everything until he has become so poor in body and soul that he must beg for his daily bread, or toil hard for it.

Each one receives, My child, according to the way he thinks and behaves.

Receive the Highest

The one who wants to receive the Highest, Me, the All-Power and the fullness, must lose his self, must give himself.

See, rich is only the one who sacrifices his personal ego for the good of humankind. My child, he will not live in the gutter nor must he live there, because he receives from My fullness and attains what is due to him as the child of his Father.

He will receive everything he needs and more, according to the natural laws of this Earth.

True wealth

True wealth is the radiance of your soul, which hears in itself the holy eternal Spirit which is one with Me, the great primordial Spirit. This child will not live in want; it will receive from My hands and partake of the great feast of life—not only in heaven, but already on Earth.

What do you lack, My child? You are not rich externally—like the rich of this world; you possess inner wealth. Whatever you need in your external life, I have given to you, and more.

See, the children in the kingdom of a spiritual life live in the fullness. People receive what they need and more, depending on the inner radiance of their soul. A human being cannot be given the complete fullness of the eternal homeland, because the Earth is dense and thus restricted by time and space. Many people live in this space and in time, and thus, the planet Earth is overpopulated. However, the one who awakens the inner radiance through a life in Me will also have enough on Earth and will not live in want.

I, the Giver

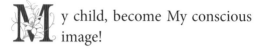y child, become My conscious image!

See, My love streams eternally! I give the forces of love unceasingly to the great totality. According to their consciousness, all entities receive My power. Each one may take from the stream of love, but each can take only as much as corresponds to their consciousness.

The consciousness of the entities can be compared to the calyx of a flower. The more the calyx opens and turns toward the sun, the more rays of the sun will enter it. See, My child, the more a person opens for My love, that is, the more selfless he becomes, the more forces he receives from My healing and My life-giving power.

Love always gives equally. Love flows for all Being: for spirit beings, human beings, souls, animals, plants and for stones. All Being receives.

The more selfless and radiating your nature becomes, the more you can receive and give from My wellspring.

My child, experience that to give is better than to take! The one who gives selflessly receives abundantly from the source of eternal love.

I Am the love

 Am the absolute love.

I see you solely as a perfect child of My love. The imperfections will lighten and be nullified through the power of the law of cause and effect, but not the absolute love.

My child, become My image!
Look at your fellow people only from My consciousness of perfect love! See them as perfect beings! Do not look at their faults and shortcomings! Forgive!

Those who behold in everything only the perfect, the beautiful and the noble see all of this with the eyes of love. And the one who views everything through My love will become truly noble and loving.

Kindness, friendliness and love draw into such a person. He is the one who could change the world to the good, insofar as the world would listen to him and delve into his self-experiences and go through their own self-experiences.

Become My image

y child, beautiful is the life in Me and with Me!

Be of good cheer: hope, love and endure! See, the angels of heaven are with you and with all My children who raise their hearts to Me and who daily cleanse their souls more of all the refuse, of the trumpery of this world.

The one who strives for the Highest will also receive from the Highest.

My child, be noble and good! Look steadfastly within and ask Me, the Lord and God, in all things.

See, I will answer you according to your consciousness, for I Am everything in all things. Recognize this!

My child, follow My instructions, then you will grow and flourish more each day!

See, My love and grace never forsake you. I, your Lord, lead you to the pinnacle of peace, where the eternal sun gives you only salvation and love.

Each soul particle needs My perfect light. If the many particles of the soul and the cells of your body are filled with light, then everything in you has been accomplished. Thus, you, too, are a cell of My body. See, it is luminous and bright; your being blossoms like the sunrise on the horizon of My life. Your senses live in Me, and I work through them. Thus, I Am consciously in you, everything in all things. See, may this knowledge give you strength and comfort in all the days filled with work as well as in those filled with privation.

The sun of righteousness is the delight of your soul. Thus, you may join in your soul's song of praise, namely: I am in God, my Father, and my Father is consciously in me. I have found and feel the perfection of my soul, the spirit body, which has again become the image of my Father. Thanks be to You, O Lord, and to Your Son.

Give thanks in joy and in sorrow

My child, learn to give the right thanks! See, in true thankfulness lies infinite joy and selflessness.

In true thankfulness, which rises from the depth of your soul to Me, the Eternal, lies true heroism. The one who gives thanks for everything, also in illness and need, awakens in Me, the Spirit of life.

Deep gratitude refreshes the soul and body. Those who give thanks forget themselves. In truly forgetting yourself, My child, My strength awakens in you, which puts everything in order and clears it up, which nullifies and erases many things.

See, I Am also mercy. Become merciful and you will become a true servant of humanity.

True service

In forgetting oneself lies true heroism, true service.

Those who are true servants of humanity do not think about money and goods. They sacrifice themselves for their neighbors.

See, this is also true heroism; this is true greatness.

True heroism

A true hero is the one who gives everything, indeed, even his life, for his sheep. Thus, have I, My child, lived, loved and given, I, your Lord and Redeemer.

Now be brave and follow Me! Bear your cross courageously and know that I will carry it with you, if you entrust yourself to Me and if you surrender to Me all your faults and weaknesses and leave them in Me, the Spirit of Christ. Come, follow Me!

Follow Me

Those who follow Me can bear much, including the accusations and insults of their fellow people. Those who consciously enter My following will not talk about the weaknesses and faults of their fellow people. Nor will they hold on to their still existing base characteristics and inclinations with brooding and fearfulness.

People who follow Me will always give, always give. They are the light in Me and I shine through them. In this way, they become capable of bearing much, and for many.

I Am the Good Shepherd. Be My sheep and become a lamb!

Become enduring

The sufferings that you presently have to bear are your own mistakes, which you have imposed on your soul during this or a former life. Now you may suffer through them.

Accept them and give thanks; for by accepting and giving thanks, you receive the strength to endure what I cannot take from you, since it is for the salvation of your soul. My child, what remains for you to endure gives you new recognitions on your path.

Endure, realize and mature; in this way you will mature toward Me and will blossom and reach full ripeness. See, I harvest only fully ripened fruit and carry it back into the glory, into the peace that the world does not know.

The world does not know Me

The world is not the Earth. The world is all that lives on the Earth and does not raise itself to God, the Eternal. This world is the worldly ones who view the planet Earth as the true and real, who can raise their horizon only as far as the clouds. Beyond that, everything is mute and deaf for them.

The one who has no eyes for Me does not see Me. The one who has no ears for Me does not hear Me. The one who has no refined sense of smell does not smell the fragrance, which streams from the life, which I Am.

A person who craves only the delights of the world does not taste what life offers him for daily consumption. He reaches for animal products because his sense of touch is not refined or noble, and does not touch what is beautiful and delicate in the light and splendor of the Godhead.

My child, I love you. My child, great is the love I have for My children.

No person can have even an inkling of My love who does not behold with his spiritual eyes the universe in all its radiance and in the manifold diversity of My life.

See, everything that exists is the expression of My love. All Being bears witness to an impersonal Creator-Spirit, which I Am.

See, My child, every movement of your body, each breath, everything that you feel and speak bears witness to a mighty, eternal, omnipresent power.

And the child who slanders Me, who takes My name in vain, who does violence to the life, see, My power is in everything—in everyone and in all things. I give it to My child, to each one in the same way. That is the impersonal love, the impersonal life.

See, from this you can surmise how great My love is. I do not strike back, I do not chastise—I give Myself in every person, in every soul, in all Being.

Just as the sun does not ask the human children: Is the way I am shining pleasing to you? Or: Is it okay for you that I shine?

See, My child, the sun gives and gives; it follows its course untiringly. It gives and gives to the moon and the stars, which, in turn, give to the Earth and the human beings. The whole solar system gives, including the Earth. It gives. See, from this you recognize in a small way the great, universal Giver, the Spirit of love.

My child and the hearts of My children that beat for Me in the right way receive more of My love since they turn their hearts to Me, just as the calyx of a flower gives itself to the sunlight, so as to absorb the sun's rays deep within itself.

Oh recognize My impersonal love! The more My child surrenders to Me, the impersonal life, and becomes impersonal itself, the more it receives from this impersonal power, from My love, until it becomes love itself, My image, and automatically shines for all people and beings, for all Being. My child, that is love: I Am, and you may be.

Become impersonal

Personality thinking, a thinking that revolves around one's own personality, is human. The more people think of themselves, of their well-being, the more limited their consciousness becomes. Those who think only of themselves are still far removed from Me, the Impersonal.

I Am the impersonal life, the fullness.
I Am who I Am in everything, also in you, My child.
I Am the fullness. I Am everything; be aware of this! The fullness, everything that exists is what I Am, and I Am in you. Are you aware of this?

If so, why do you fear people and things that are outside your high self? Through fear, you give people and things the power to dominate you.

Those who have soared into an impersonal life stand above all human emotions and inclinations; they are impersonal. They no longer think of themselves, whether this or that would be good for them. They know that they possess everything; for the fullness, I, the Impersonal, dwell in the center of their soul and in each cell of their body.

Many of My children worry about the coming time. For this reason, in this time, they have only that to which they are oriented—or much less, depending on how much doubt and fear they bring into their planning for the coming time.

Therefore, My child, the person who clings to personality thinking is limiting himself by striving to possess everything possible, to make provisions for everything that could happen in the coming time.

Free yourself from this! At all times act in accordance with the Spirit! If you know that you will depart from the temporal tomorrow, then plant a tree today for those who will remain behind, but only if you have an inner urge to do so. This is impersonal thinking and acting in the spirit of impersonal love, which sets one free.

Those who do not think of themselves, who give only out of the inner fullness—light, strength, love and good will—truly, they will have the fullness at all times and in all eternity.

Eternity is your goal

You are a child of eternity. Be aware of this!

There is no interruption to life, since everything is life. In all of infinity there is no standstill, so also not in you, in your life.

Dead are only those human beings and souls that focused all their thoughts and desires on the outside world, on matter. The heart of the soul will once again return to where its treasure is, on matter, to which it paid homage as a human being and whose pleasures and vices it considered to be its true self.

Just as constricted as the person's consciousness was, so will the soul live. Although it is a child of eternity, of infinity, it will bind itself to time and space and will lavish care and attention on these deranged thoughts, that it is a child of this world, a child of matter.

Let your consciousness soar to all the spiritual universes from Order to Mercy; link with the universal Spirit that is everything in all things. This awakens in you the thinking in terms of eternity, the awareness that feels only unending beauty and purity, that is one with all life.

The beauty
of the soul

The beauty of the soul is its purity. You attain this beauty through a noble disposition and selfless, sublime thoughts. The more selfless you become and the nobler your thoughts and your cast of mind are, the more beautiful your soul becomes.

Only beauty and the noble can flow from a beautiful, pure soul. And out of a soul filled with selfless love, only love can, in turn, flow. From a heart and a soul filled with My peace, only peace can, in turn, flow. And only harmony can flow, in turn, from harmonious people because they are filled with harmony through their indwelling love.

All that is in you finds expression in your being, which shapes your character and your behavior.

How do you find your way to
inner beauty, purity,
love and harmony?

Be aware that I, the Spirit of life, dwell in you.

I Am everything in all things. I Am who I Am, the Life. Regard everything that you behold with your inner eyes, with the eyes of the soul.

See, when you are aware that I Am the love, harmony and peace in all things, and when you meet with love everything that is, nothing contrary can happen to you. The pure and noble life will link with your pure, noble and selfless thoughts and bestow upon you more than you can imagine.

My child, trillionfold life streams toward you from all Being. That Am I, who loves you.

Keep in constant contact with Me, by day and by night. Then I Am consciously in you and you are consciously in Me.

Let love stream from your being, then you are truly a child of blessing for this world and for all Being. Then you will one day enter radiantly into My life, into eternity.

Eternity

ternity, the life, is hidden in all Being.

Let your consciousness move out to the realms of nature, to the heavenly bodies, to people, souls, beings and animals. Let your consciousness flow, flow toward the core of being that is contained in all Being.

Just as the bee betakes itself deep into the calyx of a flower, so let your consciousness penetrate deeply into all Being. Do not be content with the shell, with matter. If you are satisfied merely with the husk, you will experience the limitation of time and space again and again, since you look at the physical with physical eyes.

Let your inner being, your awakened feelings, your consciousness, stream forth deeply into the nature kingdoms, into the heavenly bodies, into all Being.

Then the core of being of life, which I Am, will open to you. You will then behold eternity, spaceless and timeless life, and feel at one with Me. Then fear and worry recede; death no longer has a shadow, because you have penetrated matter.

Death

eath is limited thinking. Death is earthly, constricted awareness.

Those who live in the face of death are already spiritually dead. They think that they live, yet they do not live. Their life is a vegetating away, an infirmity that does not end with death, but begins anew in death: vegetating away as a soul, reincarnating, vegetating away, infirmity and death. This is the fate of both soul and person, until soul and person awaken and walk the path of self-recognition.

Self-recognition
sets you free

Recognize yourself as My child; become independent of yourself and of all people, and you will be free.

A person is not able to do anything of himself. What he possesses, what he acquires, that Am I.

See, I give Myself. I Am everything in all things, also in your neighbor. I also give Myself to you through people who love you and who have taken on the task to provide for you in this life.

Therefore, never demand goods and money from anyone. Accept thankfully whatever you receive and see Me as the Giver in this.

Do not waste what you receive. Be moderate in and with all things, for what has been given to you through second or third persons, is from Me.

I serve you through your neighbor; through sun, moon and stars I serve you; through the nature kingdoms I serve you. Accept thankfully whatever you receive, for all goodness and love is from Me.

I care for you day and night. I watch over you, My child, for I, your Father, love you.

See, My child, the one who entrusts himself to Me receives. Take nothing you receive for granted. And administer well what you possess. See yourself only as a child that has received gifts! Do not hoard My gifts.

I care, I give, I help, I heal. Recognize Me in everything and accept everything thankfully, even if it seems painful to you at the moment. Know that many a soul matures through suffering.

Actualize My law, which is everything, and then you will truly receive from the fullness. Those who crave My gifts, who seize My gifts and regard them as their own, holding them and saying: "Me, me, me, only me, everything for me!"—This child will lose everything one day and will stand before Me as a beggar.

See, that is unfreedom, that is being bound and the imprisonment of the soul. Those who live in egotism, who think only of themselves, who defend the gifts I have given them and want to possess even more will become impoverished through the law of cause and effect. They will lose everything. Everything will be taken from them through the law of sowing and reaping.

One day, each soul must recognize itself. Its nakedness and exposure, its small illusory ego that must be sacrificed to become truly free in Me, the free God, the eternal Giver, who is everything in all things.

The selfless sacrifice

Do not defend yourself and do not defend anything that is merely given to you to have and administer.

Those who defend themselves and My gifts are bound. Bound people cannot liberate themselves, unless they sacrifice themselves to Me, the Eternal.

My child, sacrifice yourself through My love. See, love is the strongest power in the universe; it is always giving and always sacrificing.

Whatever you do should be imbued with selfless love. This is possible only if you do not look to the flesh but rather to the core of being of each soul.

Look through matter and link with the core of being, with Me, the Godhead. Then you behold only purity; you see only love and can give only love, because purity and love communicate with your selfless heart, and you live impersonally according to the law.

Become impersonal!

Egocentric thinking

Personality thinking is human, egocentric thinking. It is confining and self-centered. It is thinking in terms of space and time, a thinking that is not free.

Such thinking makes a person small and petty. It leads to hatred and enmity, which, in turn, leads to theft and binding, because limited ego-thinkers want only to possess everything that is worth striving for.

This selfish heart is far from Me, because it wants only to receive and not to give. This person is not a free child of the true life, but a worldly person, oriented to matter, which ultimately is nothing other than My transformed-down Spirit, transformed-down consciousness, and, in the end, My possession.

Yet, I do not think about My possession. What is Mine is also yours, and what belongs to Me belongs to you too.

Those who correctly manage their property, which is also My property, in the awareness that everything is spirit and should, in turn, be raised to the highest principle, will recognize Me, the Giver, in everything and thus, become impersonal and act accordingly.

They will no longer think of themselves but of Me, who am everything in all things.

My child, only then can the human being truly receive and become free from himself, from his personality thinking.

Become free from your self

Rely on God; trust Me in all of life's situations; be impersonal! Do not demand anything for yourself, give! One day, every human being will have to let go of everything to become free for the true journey of the soul to the light of the Godhead.

For this reason, become free! Do not bind yourself to any person; instead feel linked with each person as a unit in the filiation of God.

Become free of your self-will and practice recognizing My will. You will soon recognize My will if you examine yourself: Is your thinking still self-willed? Do you want to, or will you, surrender yourself to Me, the One who directs all things?

Examine your words! How often do you still talk about yourself? From this, too, you recognize your self-will, your egocentricity. Examine yourself, how often, when and why you defend yourself. From this, too, you recognize your ego and your self-will.

Become impersonal; become radiant! Give love and light, and you will stand in the light of your Father.

Stand in Me, in My light

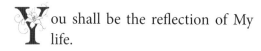ou shall be the reflection of My life.

Whatever you do, think it over. Ask yourself if Jesus of Nazareth would have acted as you would like to act. Place your thoughts, your words and your actions into the light of the Nazarene and recognize yourself in them as My child.

Give light through selflessness, and it will become light in and around you.

I Am the light. In My light nothing remains hidden. Everything will be revealed; My light will reflect everything, your good as well as your base thoughts, words and deeds. The light is the power of the seed, for without light nothing can flourish. Therefore, My light will germinate your seed, cause it to sprout and grow, until you recognize yourself in your own fruit, and then tear out the bad seed along with its taproot by way of overcoming your self.

Then it will become lighter and brighter in you and you will sow good seeds and reap good fruit. See, I take only good fruit back into the light, into My light. I do not hide the light of My child under the bushel; I place it on top of the bushel so that it may shine for many.

My child, then shine and radiate, become selfless and forget yourself, then you are served by the universe and by all those who inhabit it in pure garments of light.

Let your thoughts be the same as your words

My child, if it is possible for you to express all that you think, and if your words are the same as your thoughts, if they are the heavenly soaring music of the spheres, melodies of love that do not beguile the hearts, but awaken them and cause them to listen, then you live freely.

If your thoughts and words are lawful, then you will accomplish truly heroic deeds in My Spirit.

See, small and often trivial are the deeds of those who carry Me on their lips, but not in their hearts. These illusory deeds, which are based only on self-love and self-display, are smoke and mirrors before Me, the Absolute.

See, I have created perfect children. I cannot be effective in those who do not strive for perfection in thoughts, words and deeds.

Be heroic, willing to make sacrifices! Sacrifice yourself, your human ego, your personality thinking, your opinions, your desires, your base inclinations and longings, your personality striving.

Become impersonal! Conscious, selfless life is a divine life.

Live consciously

Whatever you do, do it totally and check your actions, whether they can be supported by Me, the Christ.

Turn away from sensual stimuli and sensual desires; strive for the higher love; then you will rise toward God's love and will link with the absolute Love, with Me, My child.

The high love is the mystical love. It is the mystical act of giving, in order to grow and to mature in the realization that love, too, has its levels from Order to Mercy.

Once you have climbed the seventh level, you have walked through all degrees of love and have worked your way up to the absolute Love, to the unification with Me, the absolute Love. Then you are truly one with Me, and you experience a high time of joy and happiness of which you have had only a partial taste on the levels to the absolute Love.

Now you truly rest in the arms of your bridegroom who draws you to His bosom both as bride and child, and who gives you the blissful kiss that weds you to Him, the great All-One, to whom you then belong for all eternity.

Become My bride

I Am your bridegroom; come, My bride, adorn yourself with the garland of virtue, with the scepter of peace, with the heroic striving to please Me completely.

Gird yourself with selfless love and ennoble yourself in all things! Distance yourself from all compulsive drives. May your striving know only one aim: purity, purity at all cost.

Exchange self-will for God's will; exchange self-love for childlike love! Surrender your base inclinations for high and noble feelings!

Sacrifice your sensual inclinations and become of like mind with Me!

My only aspiration is to unite with you, I, the purity and love itself. If this is also your striving, then you will vibrate more highly each day and you will draw closer to Me, the One who I Am from eternity to eternity.

Walk on the path of virtue and meekness. Sacrifice your passions, your egotistic thoughts; then you will hear your exalted bridegroom and you will feel, think, speak and act as He wants. Indeed, your speech and your actions will be the same as the I Am, your bridegroom. Come, My bride!

You are truly My beloved

Beloved child, listen to Me, your Father and Lord, and do as I advise you.

See, the more you live in the spirit of your Father, the closer you come to Me.

Many a child of Mine believes that I favor certain of My human children. That is human thinking and not spiritual. The Spirit of life favors none of His children. The difference lies in the fact that the one child has grown closer to My heart that flows with love than the other.

See, people in southern countries, where it is warmer than in the north, would never say they are more loved by the sun than people in the north. It is the universal law which, according to its intensity, has a different effect in the southern countries than in the northern ones. However, the sun shines equally at all times.

If you are closer to the heart of your Father through your longing and your spiritual striving for Me, then you will feel the warming and enveloping rays of My loving heart more than a child that still stands in the shadow of its feelings and passions.

Despite everything, the Spirit of love does speak to His child who is still entangled in egotism: My beloved child, come away from your limitations. Burst the armor of your human ego, so that the eternal light can shine on you and set you free from all that is human, and so that you may truly live through Me, the I Am from eternity to eternity.

I Am

Awaken daily more in Me; I Am in all Being. Observe nature in Me, the I Am. Nature lives because I Am.

Look at the stone, the minerals, with spiritual eyes. Let the primordial sensation stream from your inner being, then it will ring consciously in your inner ear: I Am the power in the stone; I Am the life.

Look at the flowers and shrubs, the trees and fruit with the inner eyes. Communicate with the inner forces that are active in all things and you will, in turn, hear Me, the breath of life of your heavenly Father, who whispers to you: My child, I Am.

I Am the sun; I Am every heavenly body. I Am the firmament and all Being. I Am nature; I Am the stone, the mineral, the flower, the shrub, the fruit.

I Am.

I Am in every little animal; I Am its life. Do not wantonly extinguish it, rather look upon it as your second neighbor. Give to it from your selfless love, for in the animal too, I Am the strength, the love and the sunniness.

Love, love, My child! Smother with love all that is base and evil. In particular, love your neighbor, your sister, your brother. See, I Am also the strength in each one of you, the Father-Mother-Spirit, the Love that wants to lead and guide the child.

Live consciously, My child, in the fulfillment of the holy laws, then your soul will soon tune in again to the inner jubilation, and the stream of the holy primordial sensation will vivify you totally.

Then you will speak consciously and feel consciously, in the deep recognition that the Father and I are one.

Only in this way, can you, and will you, love Me more than this world.

Be free of yourself

To be free of oneself means to think less and less of oneself and one's own concerns.

To be free means not to strive for property and goods, but to entrust oneself to the One who knows about all things, who is everything.

The one who is truly free is rich. And the one who is rich in his inner being does not strive for property and possessions. He has everything, and everything serves him.

This freedom cannot be acquired with money and goods, but only with a heart of gold, which does not think of itself but beats only for its neighbor.

People with golden hearts are truly happy. They are the movers of the world who bring peace into the world through selflessness and by forgetting themselves.

Become free, My child, from personality thinking, from personality feeling and wanting, then you receive what you need for your life and more.

Walk over green, fragrant pastures; they are yours. Walk over flowering meadows, through rustling woods; they are yours. Everything you see bears within the eternal Spirit, your heritage. Thus, everything is yours because the substance of all life is in you. Learn to make use of your heritage in the right way, and infinity will serve you.

Infinity, the Spirit
in all Being, serves you

Everything that is wants to serve you, the universal child, the highest life that has taken on form.

See, My child, what you see is consciousness.
The consciousness of an individual universal life has been created by Me in such a way that it serves the higher consciousness.

You, as the second-highest consciousness, as a child of God, have the gift to make the entire universal life serve you.

Subdue the Earth, thus I spoke to My own. By this I meant: When people learn to recognize and interpret the aspects of consciousness of the Earth correctly, they begin to sense what universal consciousness is, the Holy Spirit in all Being.

My child, refine your senses, make room in your inner being for all spheres of consciousness and you will learn that you are truly the highest creature after Me, your Father, since infinity, the All-consciousness, My Spirit, serves you.

Spirit is consciousness; spirit is power. I Am everything in all things, the

Spirit of your Father, the servant of all His children.

Attain this high consciousness by giving in the Giver. Give, as I give Myself eternally, I, the Spirit, the power of your Father.

I Am the Eternal, the eternal Giver.

To give makes one free

My child, you possess everything that I have. Recognize and grasp this statement in its depth.

The one who possesses everything that infinity has to offer—what else could he possibly want? Enter into your heritage by believing and trusting in Me, then your love for Me will also grow and flourish.

Recognize: Nothing happens by chance in all of infinity. Everything is well-ordered and integrated into My great law. Strive to come away from the sphere of influence of cause and effect, of sowing and reaping, then you will truly experience your heritage and you can apply it in the right way.

Yet, how small and lowly are those who are poor in spirituality! They hoard and dispute; they quarrel and complain, and yet they are poor and remain poor until they recognize their true heritage, which can be acquired only through the right humility and selflessness.

My child, accept everything as it is and do not complain! For everything that happens to you, joy and sorrow, is what you are, yourself. You are the creator of your fate, but also the conqueror of your true, eternal heritage.

Just as you present yourself, that is what you are. Just as you make your bed today—so will you sleep on it tomorrow. Realize this, My child.

See all these things in the light of Mercy and Love. These attributes of your Father show all your remaining human inclinations and impulses, so that you may sacrifice them to Me, the Eternal One, on the altar of Mercy and Love.

True sacrifice liberates; it leads to the right deed. Sacrifice your ego and enter your true eternal heritage, the universal life, which I Am—then infinity, the life, will serve you.
I Am the life.

Sacrifice

To sacrifice oneself on My altar of Love is the most difficult thing for My human children. To give up all worldly things, to gain the great whole, one needs inner greatness and trust in God.

The one who sacrifices himself initially sees nothing but smoke, the smoke of his passions and drives, of his vain thoughts and longings.

Once the smoke has lifted, then the one striving toward God initially sees nothing but ashes, the ashes of his base ego.

Now it is necessary to look in the ashes for the small smoldering ember, the Christ-light. That again means working on yourself, My child.

The one who wants to sacrifice himself to Me must now remove the ashes of his still existing, base ego and kindle the burning Christ-light, the smoldering ember of his soul, with the belief that through the Christ-light, he will come closer to Me, God, the Eternal.

This, in turn, means sacrifice. Every day, every hour and every minute, he has to pay attention to himself, to his lower thoughts that show themselves again and again, that want to rise up again and again in the human mind and eclipse the Christ-light.

With heroic sacrificial courage, he must fight against the superimposition of the soul, the still existing soul garments, the subconscious and the consciousness, until the entire root system of the human ego is removed from the field of the soul, and the brain cells register only what is noble, pure and beautiful, and the senses feel and desire only what is noble.

Recognize, My child: Then you will truly increase the Christ-light in you, which will then unite with the primordial light of your Father.

Get going on the work of great deeds! Begin, sacrifice yourself and clear up everything that still clings to you as human aspects. Then, through trust and faith, you will find your way to true love and to the unification with Me, your God and Father.

Clear up all
that moves you

My child, the human being has several aspects of will. These are the consciousness, the subconscious and the soul garments.

These aspects form the human will, the self-centered feeling, thinking and wanting.

See, My child, if you want to become free of yourself, of your base ego, then do not put off the problems that move you over and over again. Overcome them with the spiritual effort of will by surrendering to Me all that is unresolved.

Again and again, place it on My altar of Love until you are free from the problem you are struggling with. No matter how often it seems to overwhelm you, place it in good time on My altar of Love. I, your Father, will transform that part that you leave on My altar.

Keep bringing to Me those parts of your problems which, despite your sacrificial efforts, continue to bother and trouble you, until everything has been transformed by Me, your Lord and God, your Father.

See, My child, the human being will be engaged in struggle until all has been overcome by the power of My Son, the Redeemer power of Christ, until the person has freed himself from his self-centered feeling, thinking and wanting, until the consciousness and subconscious are spiritualized and the soul garments illuminated.

See, My child, soul and person must overcome these things themselves, however, with the supporting and helping Redeemer-flame, with Christ, My Son. Come and set out. Begin!

Walk with Me;
I Am your companion

Wherever you go or are, you are in the garden of Love when I, the Spirit of life, am your companion.

Walk in the awareness of God, that I Am everything in all things; then the nature kingdoms bow before you, My child, and from the thorny undergrowth that perhaps edges your path, spiritual roses grow in honor of the One who consciously goes with you, and in your honor, for you are in My image.

See everything in My consciousness. Let your consciousness flow into the minerals, into the plants and the animals and feel the unity with all forms of life, then it will be clear to you that the essence of your being is in all forms of life, and the essence of all forms of life is in you.

See, My child, if you violate an animal, your consciousness suffers and in time, you will suffer, too, because you have burdened yourself by maltreating the animal, thus damaging yourself.

Realize that whoever desecrates nature, whoever consciously inflicts suffering on animals, will one day suffer from this himself; for he violates himself and inflicts suffering on himself, since a part of his consciousness is in all life forms, and the essence of all life forms is in him, in the soul of the person.

Realize this and act accordingly! Then I shall become your conscious companion and we shall walk hand in hand through the garden of infinity, aware, My child, that what is Mine is also yours, and what is yours, that Am I, your companion. I give you a rose from heaven, it is you, yourself, My pure child. I Am the core of being and you are the jewel of the inner life, the garment of love.

I Am the Love

My love is boundless. It knows neither time nor space. All that exists is the expression of My love.

Even the evil that is expressed in this world bears within My love. See, evil could never forgive if it were only evil. In evil lie the pre-dispositions of good; in evil lies the transforming and forgiving principle, the love. Only through love does a person find forgiveness, and only through love is he forgiven.

Recognize the greatness in the almighty omnipotence of God, your

Father! The evil, bad and satanic are never only evil, bad and satanic, no matter to what degree the baseness expresses itself and rages.

In everything, in the noble and good as well as in the evil, the base, is love the maintaining and transforming principle. Thus, I Am the All-Spirit that is present in all things and that ultimately leads everything to the good, pure and noble, to Me, the Love, whose expression I Am.

Become the one who beholds

In everything I Am the universal Spirit of life. Recognize Me first in yourself, and strive for perfection, so that you again become divine, just as I created you.

If you raise your thoughts and longings to Me, the Eternal, then you will also recognize and behold Me, the life, in all things.

The worldly person's view for the Eternal is closed. Much is apparent to the spiritual person; he beholds Me, the essence of life, in all Being.

Once you recognize the essence of all Being in yourself, then you will behold yourself as a part of the universe and recognize yourself in all things.

Recognize and experience in yourself that I Am all that is noble, good and pure, for I Am the life. There is no life outside of Me. I Am everything in all things. Thus, your life, too, is the life in all things, because I Am in you and you are in Me.

Recognize yourself as part of the great totality that bears in itself all the parts of life. Thus, you are universal life out of Me. Since everything is contained in all things, you as the essence of life are also in all things.

Behold Me in you, and you behold Me in all forms of life.

If you harm your neighbor, you harm yourself, because as the essence of life, you, too, are in your neighbor. If you slander and mock your neigbor, if you rob and reject him, you are slandering and mocking yourself and at the same time, Me, since I Am in all things, as well as in your life essence. If you rob and reject your neighbor, you steal the life force from yourself and reject your true self and at the same time, Me, the I Am in all things.

If you violate the plant and animal kingdoms, you violate yourself, thus reducing your life force, which I Am.

Realize this and behold the life in all things, then you behold Me.

The truly wise one beholds people and beings, all Being, in the light of the Godhead. This is why he is illuminated and wise, since he simultaneously senses what the life is, the law. I Am the law in you, I, your Lord and God from eternity to eternity.

Be conscious of the great whole, for you are universal life, since I Am in you and you are in Me, the life.

What you think is what you are

The expression of your appearance, of your gestures and facial expressions, your clothing and how you behave, all indicate your thoughts. Those who behold you know who you are; those who merely see you do not recognize you.

For this reason, learn to recognize yourself; then you will also learn to behold. Then you will behold the people and things with the eyes of the Spirit, to whom all things are revealed. As long as you still merely see, you look only at the external appearance. You pass sentence on the external; you judge because you do not recognize yourself.

The one who passes sentence and makes judgments can be certain that something similar exists in himself. The one who writes off his neighbor has in himself what he condemns in his neighbor or maliciously attributes to him.

Recognize yourself in your neighbors. How you think about them, what you think of them, this is what you are, yourself. But the one who beholds has explored himself and beholds the people and things with the inner eyes of Mercy, with the expression of understanding, of good will, of understanding love.

Become a beholder!

"The Father and I are one"

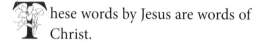

These words by Jesus are words of Christ.

"The Father and I are one" means: *one* spirit, *one* life, *one* truth and *one* love.

See, child, one day each soul will find this oneness with Me through My eternal grace. Practice so that your thinking, feeling, wanting and acting may become like Me, then you will reach the one stream that knows about all things, that beholds all things, that is all Being, God.

Become divine, become impersonal. Forget yourself; then you gain Me, the impersonal One.

Think less and less of your small ego; instead, let yourself be guided by Me, then you will gain Me. Do not interrupt when others are speaking; be calm, be impersonal. Remain linked with Me, then I, the eternal power, will become active in you and your words will carry weight and be powerful for all those who speak much and trivially. Be free of your self, then your word will be My word.

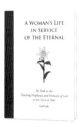

A Woman's Life in
Service of the Eternal

My Path as
the Teaching Prophetess
and Emissary of God
at this Turn of Time
Gabriele

In her autobiographical descriptions, Gabriele gives us a lively insight into her development as a human being and her calling to become the prophetess of God—and what it means to bring His Word, His Love and Wisdom to the Earth at this time.

204 pp., HB, ISBN: 978-3-89201-814-8

Gabriele Publishing House – The Word
P.O. Box 2221, Deering, NH 03244, USA
North America: Toll-Free No. 1-844-576-0937
International Orders: +49-9391-504-843
www.Gabriele-Publishing-House.com